Afriku

Adjei Agyei-Baah

Afriku

© 2016 Adjei Agyei-Baah
Translation © 2016 Adjei Agyei-Baah
Translation Editor: Eric Antwi (Ghana)
Introduction © 2015, 2016 Hidenori Hiruta
Cover Design: John Amankwaah (Ghana)

ISBN 9798628845295

Red Moon Press
PO Box 2461
Winchester VA
22604-1661 USA
www.redmoonpress.com

second printing

Dedication

*My pleasure for your leisure—
It's for you, Africa—
Celebrate!*

A Guide to the Pronunciation of Twi

/aa/ as in **a**rm
/ae/ as in **a**y**e**
/ɔ/ as in c**au**ght
/ɔɔ/ as in c**a**ll
/ee/ as in p**a**ge
/ei/ as in fr**ay**
/ea/ as in p**edia**trics
/eɛ/ as in f**ea**r
/ɛ/ as in st**e**p
/ɛɛ/ as in h**e**rb
/ɛe/ as in f**e**d
/hw/ as in **wh**eel
/hy/ as in **sh**ed
/io/ as in k**io**sk
/ia/ as in cav**ea**t
/ie/ as in f**ie**rce
/oa/ as in k**oa**la
/oɔ/ as in pl**o**d
/oo/ as in t**o**ll
/kw/ as in **qu**ality
/ky/ as in **ch**ief
/gy/ as in **gy**m
/nw/ as in **nu**de
/ny/ as in **ni**l
/tw/ as in **tw**eed
/ua/ as in T**ua**reg
/ue/ as in P**ue**rto Rico
/uo/ as in b**uoy**

Foreword

Adjei Agyei-Baah is the winner of the Akita Chamber of Commerce and Industry President Award in the English section of the 3rd Japan-Russia Haiku Contest. The award-giving ceremony was held as part of the international haiku conference at the Akita International University in Japan, October 25, 2014. Adjei delightedly spoke with attendees via Skype to share a word or two with the audience and other participants when he received his award from the president of the Akita Chamber of Commerce and Industry.

Akito Arima, the president of the Haiku International Association in Tokyo, Japan, was very delighted to hear that Adjei would spread haiku further because of its brevity and its coexistence with nature, and that he would continue to read and to delve deep into haiku aesthetics and get back to us someday with good news to share.

A few months after the president heard these good intentions, to my great delight, I excitedly received the news from Adjei that he was going to publish a haiku collection, strongly believing haiku is a beautiful genre which can be used to tell their African story and wonderful settings. He intuitively and creatively describes his natural surroundings in haiku, the shortest form of poetry. For example, he takes up in his haiku "harmattan, egret, kapok, mango, Afadjato, cocoa, eagle, and cocoyam as the objects in nature that are particularly interesting and influential to him in his surroundings.

He wrote this haiku about harmattan (a dry dusty wind that blows along the northwest coast of Africa) in his haiku collection *Afriku*

> harmattan peak
> not only does trees' bark crack
> the heels too!

He also describes what he sees in his daily life in his own way of writing haiku or senryu from his own viewpoint:

> pavement beggar—
> on his lips
> the footprints of harmattan

Here is an excerpt from *Asahi Haikuist Special* by David McMurray, professor at The International University of Kagoshima in Japan, November 17, 2014.

Akito Arima, an avid haikuist and former education minister, addressed academics at the Akita International University in an effort to convince them that haiku should be added to UNESCO's Intangible Cultural Heritage list. He reassured students in the audience that haiku can be composed by everyone, from the man in the street to the likes of Swedish poet Tomas Tranströmer, the Nobel laureate of literature in 2011 who penned at age 23: disappearing deep in his inner greenness / artful and hopeful. Later in his career he penned in Swedish:

My happiness swelled
and the frogs sang in the bogs
of Pomerania

By stressing that haiku can deepen mutual understanding and enjoyment of different cultures between those people who read or compose the poem, Arima garnered support for his idea that "haiku can help make the world peaceful."

Adjei Agyei-Baah has great interest of pioneering this art, haiku, in his country and further takes it up as his Phd thesis (*Haiku in Africa*). Haiku tells their African stories and wonderful settings in nature, and also connects people in the most wonderful way we can think of. Adjei's haiku is in truth beneficial for us, mankind:

morning dew—
perhaps heaven weeps
for mankind

—*Hidenori Hiruta, February 2015*

Afriku

old pond—
the living splash
of Bashō's frog

(for & after Bashō)

sutae dadaa—
nkaedum a Bashō
apotrɔ gyaeɛ

**drought—
the farmer digs
into his breath**

ɛpɛbrɛ
okuani fɔmtuo
si ne homee mu

roasting sun
an egret's measured steps
in buffalo shadow

owia branee
nantwinoma tutu nanamɔn
wɔ nantwie sunsum mu

leafless tree
lifting a cup of nest
into the sky

dua kwatrekwa
a apagya anoma prebuo
de kyerɛ soro

wooden doll —
the dry laughter
of an African child

aboduaba anim —
abibirem abɔfra
serewe ɛ

one crow dead
a thousand caws
make the funeral

sɛ kwaakwaadabi
wu a, kwaa kwaa apem na
wɔde yɛ no ayie

dead crows
hanging as scarecrows —
the bogeyman's farm

nkwaakwaadabi
a ɛsensɛn ho sɛ ɔberekutu —
samantefie afuom

faggots on fire
the shadow of a spider
slips out of the hearth

gyentia ɛredɛre
ananse sunsum dwane firi
asomorofi mu

season of migration
the lightning dash
of a late egret

atukɔberɛ
nantwinoma bi a waka akyiri
mmirikatɛntɛ

old fighter jet
in a movie sky
two bound dragonflies

ako adupre dadaa
ahudede mmienu a
woaka afuam

gust of wind . . .
the crow takes off
in a zigzag line

ahum mframa
kwaakwaadabi atufaa
afumpaa

traffic holdup
the absurdity of politics
served fresh on the
airwaves

kwanso dwoodwoo
amanyɔsɛm mu akomasɛe
te atese wɔ kasafidie so

refusing to board his school bus
he exclaims:
"teacher says I'm not a gentleman"

"tikya se mennyɛ ɔkrakyeni"
m'abofra pem so sɛ
ɔremforo sukuu lɔre

honeymoon night
the horn of a midnight train
initiates another round

awareɛ ahosɛpɛ da
anadwofa keteke abɛn
hyɛ yɛn sɛ yɛnni dɔ

school memories—
all the farts concealed
by shifting my chair

sukuu nkaeɛ bi
mframabɔne a mede sieeɛ wɔ
m'akonnwa twetwee mu

morning dew—
perhaps heaven weeps
for mankind

anɔpa bosuo—
sɛsɛɛ ɔsoro su gu
adasa so

riverbank—
two swallows compete
dipping tails

sutene ano
asomfena mmienu de wɔn to
boro asuo

egrets in formation
a young one
breaks the rule

sutene ano
asomfena mmienu de wɔn to
boro asuo

abandoned communication kiosk
Jesus on the phone
speaking!

nkratoɔ adaka a
yɛayi no totwene, yesu nfonin a wɔne
n'agya rekasa

lonely
as I canoe by . . .
the moon

ankonam
wɔ berɛ a mede kodoɔ retwam—
osram

creaking joints
he fondles the medal
of his youth

apɔso mmerɛyɔ
wɔde ne mmerante berɛm
abasobɔdeɛ kyekyere ne werɛ

dawn —
the distant sound
of my neighbor's broom

dasuom —
prayɛ nne a ɛfiri
akyiri

Mother's Day—
one deep enema
still rings a bell

εnanom da
me werε remfiri bεntoa bi a
me na de gyinaa me

distant cry . . .
the heartfall
of a mother

abofra nteamu
ɛna akoma
te tɔ ne yam

disputed land—
crows flout
the borderlines

manso asaase
nkwaakwaadabi di mu
ahyemfire

first sail . . .
inside his paper boat
the weight of water

n'akwantuo a ɛdi kan
ne krataa hyɛma mu—
nsuo mu duro

castle cannons—
pointing where
their owners have gone

Oguaa abankɛseɛm
Ngresifoɔ atubra rekyerɛ
wɔn akyiri kwan

full moon—
the scarecrow watches
its own shadow

ɔsram a apue
afuom kaakaamotobi a
ɔrebɔ ne sunsum ho ban

dark moon—
the shriek of an owl
unsettles a dream

osram a ahinta
ɔpatuo bi nteamu maa me bɔɔ
pitiri wɔ daeɛ mu

pavement beggar—
on his lips
the footprints of harmattan

nkwankyen srɛsrɛni
ɔpɛ agya n'anammɔn
wɔ n'ano ho

dawn rivalry—
a muezzin
and a rooster

ahemanakye akansie
kramokokonini
ne akokɔnini

noisy corn mill—
the operator's son
in a peaceful slumber

nikanika dan mu
ɔyamfoɔ ba a wada
nnahɔɔ

mama's soup—
trying to adjust
to my wife's

ɛna nkwan
mebɔ mmɔden sɛ
me yere deɛ bɛtere m'anom

**end of the month
that pleasant smell
of payday**

bosome awieeɛ
mframa papa bi a ɛbɔ wɔ
akatua da

stone meal . . .
mother fakes supper
to put the kids to sleep

anwumere aduane
maame de boɔ si gya so
de deda mmofra

misty morning
a crow trying a balance
on a church pinnacle

anɔpa bɔ
kwaakwaadabi a ɔrepɛ nyinasoɔ
wɔ asɔre dadepɔn so

stillness—
vibrating the silence
the woodpecker's knock

kommyɛ
abobɔnua woso
dinn yɛ

Carol's night—
stuck in the prisoner's throat
a broken halleluiah

buronya nwomtoɔ
haleluya ka ɔdeduani
menem

childhood memories
the wood shavings that light
up
mother's charcoal

mmofra berem nkaeɛ bi
dua atentenhuo a na ɛna
de sɔ ne bidie

country windmill
slowly blending breeze
and sunlight

akurase bɔmframa
a ɛreyam mframa
ne owia kanea

village night out
the lamps of fireflies
everywhere

akurase anadwo nanteɛ
bogya nkanea
te atese

communal vigil—
exploring both sides of darkness
fireflies

mpotam apɛsiri
bogya di anadwom
ahyemfire

back and forth
shadows of leaves brush
the face of the moon

nhahan sunsum
a ɛredi akoneaba
popa osram anim

evening lull
smoke curling up
from an easy chair

towia wisie
a ɛrepagya ne mu
afiri ahodwo akonnwam

vacant anthill—
the final luster
of a cobra's shed skin

esie a aguo
owia kanea a ɛredum
wɔ ɔpramire howorɔ mu

morning moon—
the lateness of the sun
in shifting

ɔsram a apue anɔpa
owia twentwɛn ne–nan ase
wɔ ne nsesaeɛ mu

Father's Day
all he asks for is
a pipe and easy chair

agyanom da
nea ɔrebisa ara ne
abua ne ahodwo akonnwa

**garden reading
a ripe mango drops
with a splash of red ants**

afikyifuom akenkan
amango te tɔ fam
pete ntatea kɔkɔɔ

deserted shore
the wind sharpens its voice
over a conch

mpoano a atae dinn
mframa se ne nne
wɔ sunam hankra mu

a pause
in my dream
mosquito bite

pitiribɔ
wɔ me daeɛ mu—
ntontom ka

an early bird
at the tail of a late worm
first light

dasuom anoma a
wasɔ sonson duapom —
anɔpa hann

windy mountain
praying in tongues with me
a tattered flag

bepɔso mframa—
frankaa bi a ateteɛ
ne me ka kasahorɔɔ

a leaf falls
into its shadow
onto itself

ahahan te tɔ
ne sunsum mu
tɔ n'ankasa so

harmattan peak
not only does the tree's bark crack
the heels too!

ɔpeberɛ mpɔmpɔnsoɔ
ɛnyɛ nnua abena nko ara na
ɛpaepae, nantini nso ka ho

all that remain
of a lost tribe's story—
scratches and scars

nkaedum a ɛgyina hɔ
ma abusuakuo bi a wɔn ase—
ahye ntitiyɛ ne nkotwa

jazz night
the thin line between
sax and sex

anwummerɛ nnedaeɛ nnwom
ɔkwanteaa a ɛda sankuo
ne ɛnna mu

dozing on a bus
the head of a passenger
tilts for a kiss

ɔre mu nna
ɔkwantuni de ne tiri
bɛpɛ mfeano

shea butter market
sellers hold the sun
in water sprinkles

nkuto dwom
adetɔnfoɔ de nsupete
kyekyere owia

harmattan winds . . .
crossing the border
with leaves

ɔpɛbere mframa
tase nhahan de twa
ɛhyeɛ

again they twinkle —
new stars beaten out
of an old moon

biom ɛgu nhyerɛne —
nsoroma foforɔ a waboro
afiri bosome dada mu

this lunchtime
more protein in my beans —
weevils

awia ɛdidie
ahocden mmorosoɔ me nya —
atedua mu mmoa

back to school—
chalk markings on the board
refuse a wipe

akwamma awieeɛ—
atwerɛ a wɔgyaa no atwerɛpono so
popa yɛ den

roadside beggar
he waits for the traffic light
to turn red

nkwankyɛn srɛsrɛfoɔ
ɔretwɛn sɛ trafik
bɛsɔ kɔkɔɔ

plastic flowers—
your long-gone fragrance
I pretend to nurse

nhwiren dada
wo ho hwam mmerɛ bi
na mede kyekyere me werɛ

kind bartender—
he lifts a drunkard's head
to wipe the table

nsahyɛfoɔ bi ayamuyɛ—
ɔpegya sadweam tiri
popa ne pono so

just a moment—
distant lightning connects
sky and earth

mmerɛ tiawa—
akyirikyiri ayerɛmo
ka ɔsoro ne asaase bom

jungle shot
the scattered leaves
of birds

kwaem tutoɔ
nhahan te pete sɛ
nnomaa a wɔretu

distant thunder
the peal of one valley
transferred to the next

akyirikyiri agradaa
to ne nne firi eku baako mu
kɔ ku foforɔ mu

mountain walk . . .
only our shadows
dare the cliffs

bepɔso panteɛ
yɛn sunsum nko ara
na ɛyɛ mmarimasɛm

moving water
causing stagnant water
to move

nsutene
kɔbɔ nsutae mu
ma no tu tene

rock ledge—
a wolf inhales
the moon

ɔbotanso
sakraman twe osram
wura ne homee mu

two stuck dogs
untying their knot
end of mating season

ahosɛpɛ awieeɛ
nkraman mmienu
pere ntemu

dry season
the dam shows the ribs
of its depth

ɛpɛbarɛ
anyinam ahweɛ
da ne nkrampan adi

shoreline
my footprints
go to sea

mpoano
m'anamɔn
yera gu po mu

tripping on the escalator
the new migrant
introduces himself

atwedeforo ntehweε
ɔmanfrani da
ne ho adi

the slow approach
to the pond—
frogs take back their eyes

mpɔtorɔ mem wɔn ani
bere a merepini
nsutae bi ho

my neighbor
I cannot wake:
his tap drips all night

me fipanni
a merentumi nnyane no—
ne nsuo bugu anadwosuom

riverside
a crocodile waits
in a monkey shadow

nsutene ho
ɔdɛnkyɛm a wahinta
wɔ asoroboa sunsum mu

lecturer's wife
how long must her husband
sleep sleeplessly

ɔkyerɛkyerɛni yere
nkosi daben na ne kunu
nna korɔkorɔ

sleepless night
caught between her snore
and my toothache

nnakorɔkorɔ
megye me ho gyena
wɔ me kaka mu
ne ne nkorɔmo tuom

paying the driver's mate
with my last torn money
my son points it out

mede sika a ateɛ
retua hyɛma toɔ —
me ba yi me ma

black coffee
white sugar
I stir the world into oneness

kɔfe tuntum
asikyire fufuo
meka wiase bom baako

a dragonfly pausing the wind

ahudede a ɔregyina mframa

smiling pond . . .
a dragonfly dips
its tail

tadeɛ ɛresere
ahudede de ne dua
bom

night river
bringing him closer
the boy on the moon

anadwo sutene
twe abofra a ɔte ɔsram
so ba fam

mining town
on the surface of buildings—
worry lines

sikakɔkɔɔ kuro
ɛdan biara anim
amunamuna

end of the road—
a railway track runs
into the earth

ɔkwan awieeɛ
keteke nnadeɛ
wura fam

Acknowledgements

First of all, I am most grateful to God for his talent given to me and also to the following personalities for their diverse roles played to bring this debut collection to completion: Pansiwaa, my kindhearted wife for her understanding and granting me more space to pursue my haiku dream. Aubrie Cox, editor of *Frogpond*, who first handed me her personal haiku notes and edited all my early written pieces when I first came in as a novice to the haiku table. Mr. Anatoly Kudryavitsky, editor of *Shamrock*, who gave me my first journal publication in 2011. I remember that night so well, and quite remember opening the site hundred times till the next day. Also to Kala Ramesh, a kindhearted teacher and mother, whose passion to help upcoming haiku poets had always inspire me to help young haiku poets in my part of the continent. Gillena Cox, a mother and personal friend for sharing haiku thoughts and moments with me. Mr. John Tiong Chunghoo, a good friend and fine haiku poet whom I became attach to at the beginner of my haiku career.

Emmanuel Kalusian, my co-partner and a talented African haijin at Africa Haiku Network, for his encouragement and sharing my dream in our quest of promoting haiku art in Africa. Alan Summers, a haiku teacher and friend who has always provided me with thoughts and resources in times of need. Robert D. Wilson, founder and owner of *Simply Haiku* for his rich haiku archives which had been of immense help to me in my haiku journey. Mr. Jim Kacian, founder of The Haiku Foundation and owner of Red Moon Press, for his mega-THF haiku archive which had served as my personal library and as well trusting in my maiden collection to give it a 'Red Moon Press' seal. Kristjaan Panneman, owner of *Carpe Diem Haiku Kai* for his rich daily haiku tutorial at his site and inspiring me to become a blogger. Hidnenori Hiruta, the administrator of *Akita Haiku International Network* for writing the foreword and also paving the way for me to become the Winner of Akita Chamber of Commerce and Industry President Award (in the English section) at the 3rd Japan-Russia Haiku Contest, 2014. and to Prince K. Mensah,

Jacob Kobina Ayiah Mensah, Nana Fredua-Agyeman, Celestine Nudanu, Ali Znaida, Barnabas Ìkéolúwa Adélékè, Emmanuel-Abdalmasih Samson, Nshai Waluzimba, Caleb Mutua, and Patrick W. Wafula, etc. my contemporary Afriku/haiku brethren, for their unwavering passion and commitment for the growth of the art, and leaving trails for the generations to come. To the young and fierce upcoming ones like, Kwaku Feni Adow, Kojo Adu Turkson, Prah Justice Joseph, Gordon Ayisi, Sarpong Kumankuma, etc. who are grooming themselves in the closet and wait patiently to burst into full-fledged afriku ambassadors. To Emmanuel Ofosu Agyemang a brother and the co-founder of Poetry Foundation Ghana who had always trusted in my talent and assured me of greatness. To Mr. Eric Antwi, my colleague tutor at Serwaa Nyarko Girls Senior High School who reviewed my Twi translation and also the warmest appreciation to Mrs. Harriet Hedoti Wiafe, a colleague tutor in the same institution who had many times read through my haiku and shared thoughts with me.

And also want to extend my profound gratitude to my haiku godfathers and inspirers: Prof. Richard Gilbert, Kumamoto University, Japan, for his review of my book and sharing intimate thought with me on my haiku career. Prof David McMurray, editor of the *Asahi Haikuist Network*, for his kind thought of helping me to deepen my knowledge haiku. Dr. Mawuli Adjei, the author of *Testament of Season* and *The Jewel of Kabibi*, for his motivation and being there for me all the time. Dr. Wanjohi Wa Makokha, Kenyan poet and critic and the author of *Nest of Stones*, (2010), for his trust in me to championing African haiku. Roundsquare Chumolet, Jokesmith at the "University of Mosquitoes", Kenya, a friend at heart who provided the oil to light the Afriku torch! And lastly, a 'tonful' of appreciation to the following personalities (siblings and friends) who funded the production of the book *Afriku*:

Anthony Sarpong (US)
Michael Owusu Gyimah (Canada)
Thomas Adjei Afriyie (US)
Gifty Adjei (US)

Special Mention

Recognition is also due to the editors and publishers of the following journals in which some of the poems in this collection first appeared: *Shamrock, World Haiku Review, Frogpond, Acorn, Cattails, Paper Wasp, Failed Haiku, The Heron's Nest, Brass Bell Journal, Chrysanthemum, Wild Plum, Asahi Hakuist Network, Akita Haiku International Network, One Hundred Gourds, The Living Haiku Anthology, Africa Haiku Network, Akitsu Haiku Quarterly Journal, Naad Anunaad Anthology* 2016, etc.

ADJEI AGYEI-BAAH lives in Kumasi (Ghana) and is a part-time university lecturer. He is a co-founder of Poetry Foundation Ghana and Africa Haiku Network. In 2015, he co-launched the *Mamba Journal*, Africa's first international haiku journal with Emmanuel Jesse Kalusian. Adjei is the champion of "Afriku", a haiku form which seek to project the unique images, symbols and rhythm of Africa for global delight and attention. In 2009, he organized Poetry Aloud programmes in some selected senior high schools in Ghana, leading to the birth of *Poetry Ink*, Ghana's first poetry anthology for senior high school students. Adjei is winner of several international awards, and a contributor to several anthologies. And his poems has also appeared in several international magazines and journals such as *Frogpond* (US), *The Heron's Nest* (US), *Paper Wasp* (Australia), *Shamrock* (Ireland), *Acorn* (US), *World Haiku Review* (Japan), *Cattails* (US), *Asahi Haikuists Network* (Japan), *One Hundred Gourds* (Australia) as well as various blogs and internet publications. His piece "For the Mountains" was selected by the BBC in a Poetry Postcard project to represent Ghana in the 2014 Commonwealth Games held in Glasgow, Scotland. He is a member of many haiku groups online and has published in world anthologies *Naad Anunaad Haiku Anthology* (2016) and *Cherry Blossom – Bulgaria* (2016). He was the Chief Haiku Judge at Babishaiku Poetry Award 2016, Uganda and invited guest poet at My Haiku Pond Academy (Netherland), 2016 and Carpe Diem Haiku Kai (Netherland), 2015. He is the author of *Afrikuland* <www.afrikuland.blogspot.com> and can be reached at <kwakubaaa@gmail.com>.

Made in the USA
Middletown, DE
15 November 2024